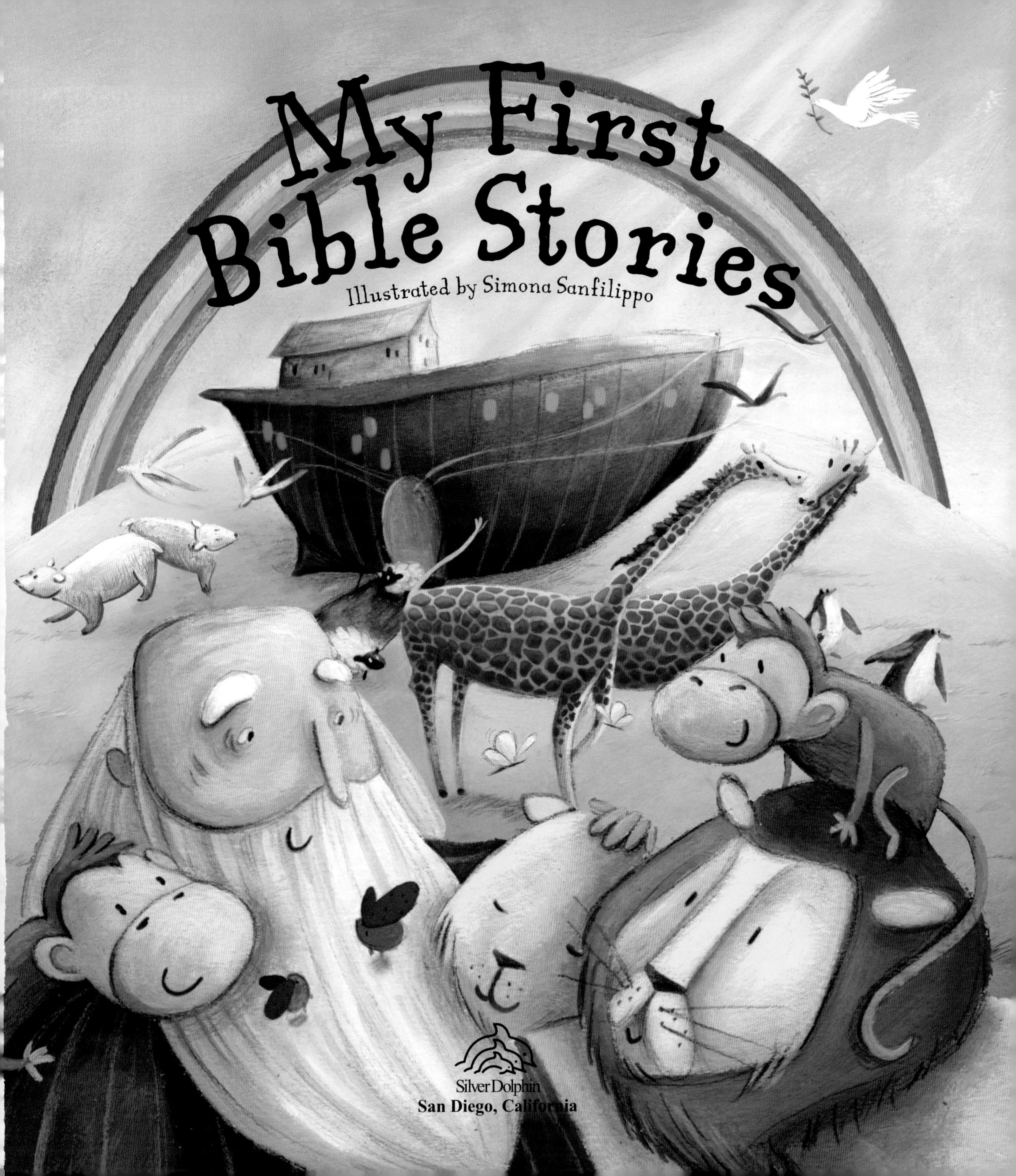

My First Bible Stories
Illustrated by Simona Sanfilippo
Silver Dolphin
San Diego, California

Silver Dolphin Books
An imprint of the Baker & Taylor Publishing Group
10350 Barnes Canyon Road, San Diego, CA 92121
www.silverdolphinbooks.com

Consultant: Fiona Moss RE Adviser, RE Today Services
Editor: Cathy Jones
Designer: Chris Fraser

ISBN-13: 978-1-60710-795-8
ISBN-10: 1-60710-795-3

Library of Congress Cataloging-in-Publication data available upon request.

Manufactured, printed, and assembled in Guangdong, China.
1 2 3 4 5 16 15 14 13 12

CONTENTS

Noah's Ark

Old man Noah was a very good man.

He loved God and always listened to what God told him. God loved Noah because he was good.

But God was not happy with the rest of the people. They didn't listen and behaved very badly.

One day, God said to Noah, "I am going to flood the earth to wash it clean. Build a wooden ark and make sure it will not leak.

“Take your family and two of every kind of animal into the ark.

Bring plenty of food for everyone. In seven days I will make it rain.”

So Noah did as God told him.
His sons Shem, Ham,
and Japheth helped.

They chopped
down trees.

They hammered
in pegs.

They sawed big planks

They painted
the ark so that it
would not leak.

They all worked very hard until the ark was finished.

But there was no time to rest.
Next, they collected two of every kind
of animal. It wasn't easy!

Two by two the
animals crept or slithered
or plodded or hopped onto the ark.

They made a terrible noise!

And when they were all inside, God shut the door.

Sure enough, after seven days, it began to rain.
Drip, drop—the rain didn't stop!
The water rose and lifted the ark.

For forty days and forty nights it rained. Even the highest mountains were flooded.

Inside the ark it was dark.
All the animals squashed
together and
they made
a terrible
noise!
Squawk!
Moo!

But Noah trusted God and knew they were all safe and dry.

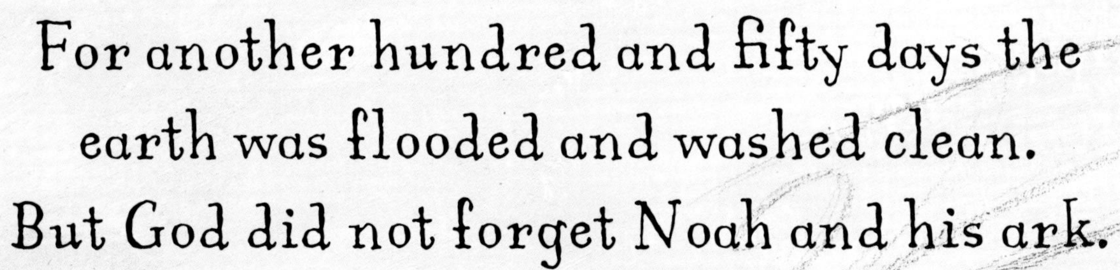

For another hundred and fifty days the
earth was flooded and washed clean.
But God did not forget Noah and his ark.

Then God sent a wind
and the flood went down.
Finally, the ark landed on the
top of the highest mountain.

Slowly, the water went down and down. Noah opened the window and saw other mountaintops.

He sent out a dove, but the dove soon flew back.

A week later,
Noah sent out
the dove again.

This time it flew back
carrying a twig in its beak.

Noah waited another week
and sent out the dove again.

This time it didn't fly back. At last,
the dove had found dry land.

Then God said to Noah,
"It's safe to come out now."

Two by two, the animals
came out of the ark into
the sunshine.

Noah thanked God
for keeping them all safe.

After that, God made a promise to Noah never to flood the earth again.

As a sign of his promise,
God put a colorful rainbow in the sky.

Next Steps

Look back through the book to find more to talk about and join in with.

* Copy the actions: do the actions with the characters—chop, saw, hammer, and paint; or creep, slither, plod, and hop.
* Join in with the rhyme: pause to encourage joining in with "Drip, drop—the rain didn't stop!"
* Counting: match the pairs of animals, counting one penguin, two penguins.
* Colorful rainbow: name the colors of the rainbow together, then look back to spot the colors on other pages.
* All shapes and sizes: describe the animals in terms of shape or size. Look for a tall giraffe, a tiny mouse, a fat elephant, and a long snake.
* Listening: when you see the word on the page, point and make the sound—Moo! Squawk! Oink! Sssssss! Growl! Baa! Squeak!

Now that you've read the story . . . what do you remember?

* Who told Noah to build the ark?
* Why did God send the flood?
* What went into the ark?
* How long did it rain?
* Where did the ark come to rest?
* Why did God send the rainbow?

What does the story tell us?
If we listen to God, he will look after us.

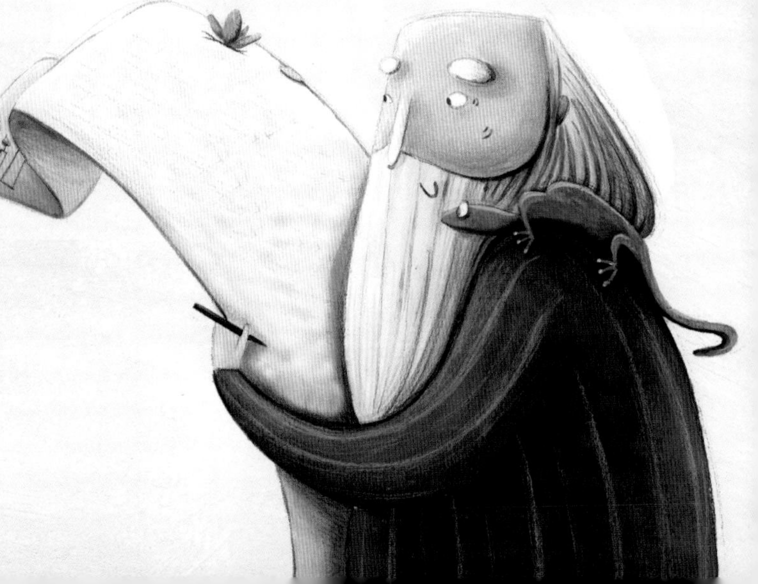

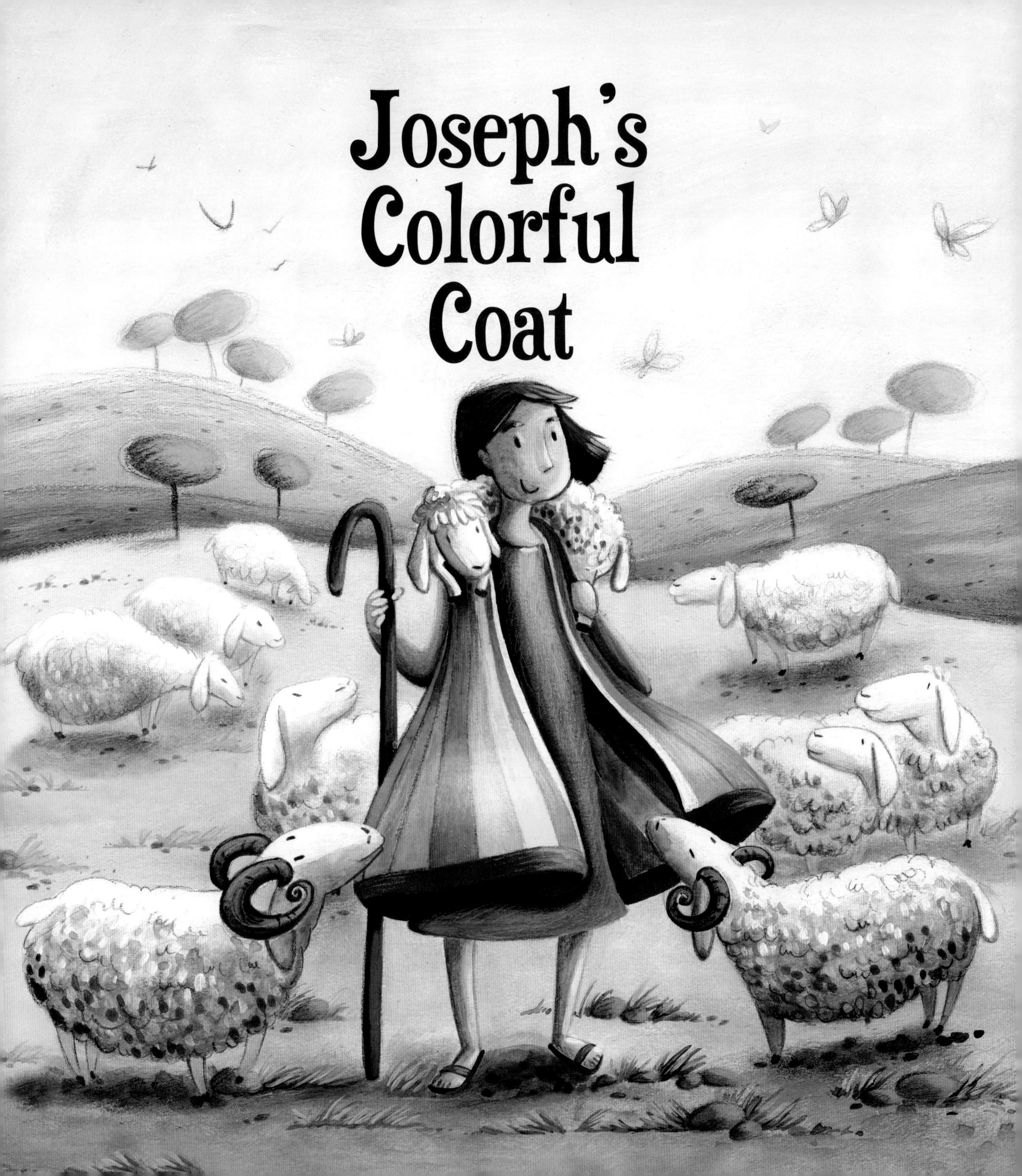
Joseph's
Colorful
Coat

Long ago, Joseph's father, Jacob, gave him a colorful new coat. This made Joseph's brothers angry.

Joseph was younger than his eleven brothers.

"Why does he get a new coat and we don't?" grumbled one brother.

"He's always the favorite," complained another.

One night, Joseph had two dreams.

In the first dream, eleven bundles of wheat gathered around Joseph's bundle and bowed.

In the second dream, the sun, moon, and eleven stars bowed to Joseph.

When Joseph told his brothers about the dreams, they were angry.

"Do you think we are going to bow to you?" they asked.

Soon after, Joseph went to find his brothers. They were still annoyed with him. When they saw him coming, they said, "Let's kill him and pretend a wild animal attacked him."

But brother Reuben tried to save him.
"Let's just leave him in this empty well.
If we tear his coat, Father will think he is dead."

Just then, some merchants
came riding by with camels.
They were on their way to Egypt.

Brother Judah hatched another plan. "Let's sell Joseph to the merchants as a slave."

And that's what they did.

The brothers went home and showed their father Joseph's torn coat. Jacob thought that Joseph was dead. He was very sad.

But Joseph was on his way to Egypt to be sold as a slave.

Joseph became a slave of one of the king's officers. For a long time he was happy and trusted by his master.

But the master's wife tricked him and he went to jail.

Two men were in the jail with Joseph.

The first man said, "I had a dream—
what does it mean?
I squeezed three
grapevines
into the king's cup."

Joseph said happily,
"God knows what your
dream means. In three days, the king
will send for you to be his wine servant."

The second man said, "I had a dream—what does it mean? I had three baskets of bread, but birds came and pecked the bread."

Joseph said sadly, "God knows what your dream means. In three days you will die."

Both dreams came true.

Then, one day, the king had two dreams. In the first dream, seven skinny cows ate seven fat cows!

In the second dream, seven straggly cornstalks ate seven strong cornstalks!

When the king told his dreams to the wise men, they were puzzled.

But then the king's wine servant said, "I know someone who can tell you what your dreams mean. His name is Joseph."

The king sent for Joseph. He said: "I had two dreams, what do they mean?" And he told Joseph his dreams.

Joseph said, "God knows what your dreams mean.

Seven fat cows and seven strong cornstalks
mean seven years of good harvest.

Seven skinny cows and seven straggly cornstalks
mean seven years of bad harvest."

"Oh, no! What will we do?"
asked the king.

"Save wheat from
the good harvest
to feed the people
during the
bad harvest,"
said Joseph.

The king was so pleased that he put Joseph in charge.

For seven years the harvest was good, and they kept some wheat.

For the next seven years the harvest was bad, but the people had plenty to eat.

Far away, Joseph's father and brothers were hungry. "Oh, no! What will we do?" they cried.

"We will go to Egypt—they have plenty of food," said Jacob.

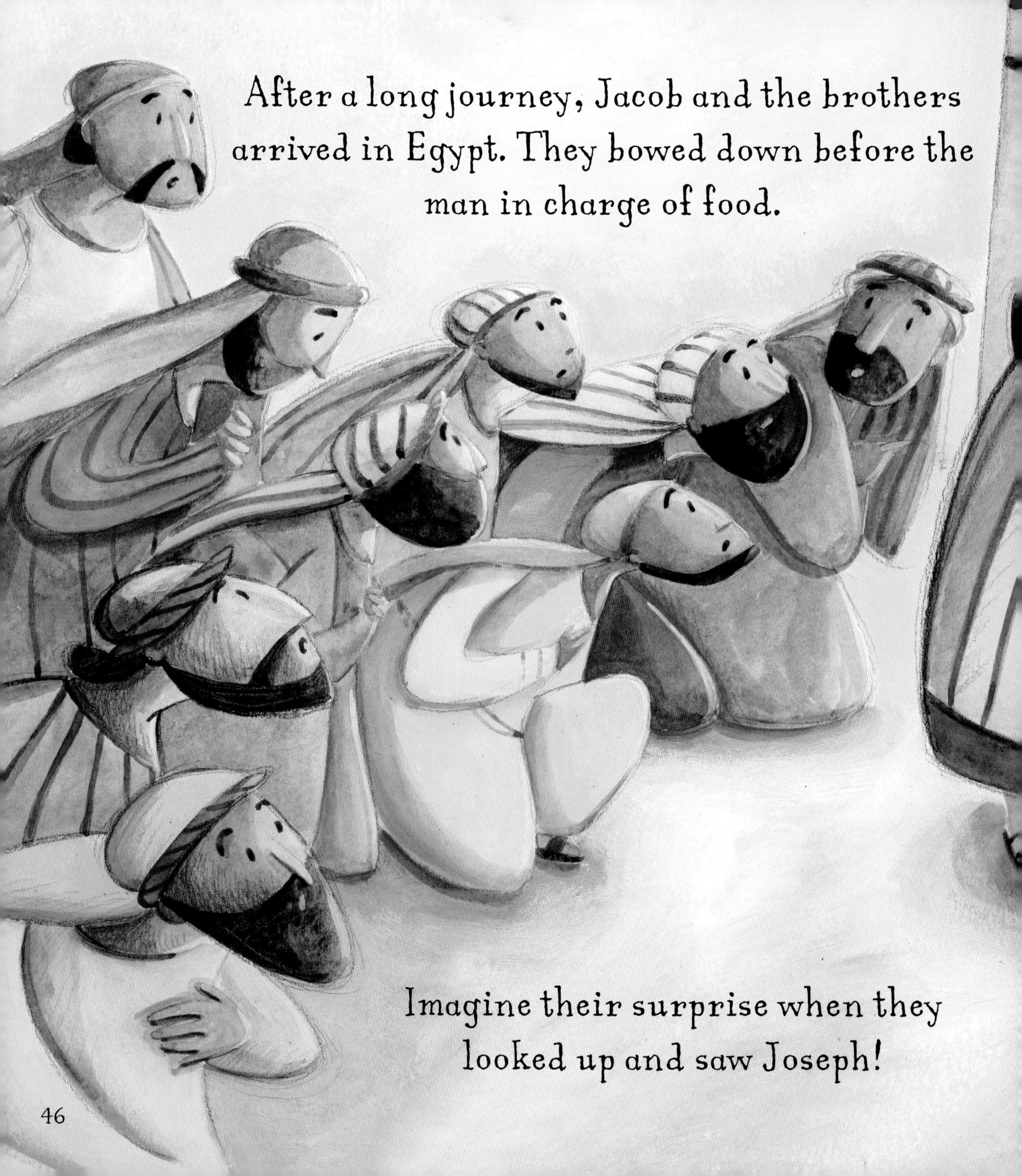

After a long journey, Jacob and the brothers arrived in Egypt. They bowed down before the man in charge of food.

Imagine their surprise when they looked up and saw Joseph!

Joseph was pleased to see his father and brothers after all these years. The dream he had had all those years ago had come true.

Next Steps

Look back through the book to find more to talk about and join in with.

* Copy the actions: be a bundle of wheat bowing down, or be a twinkling star.
* Join in with the rhyme: pause to encourage joining in with "I had a dream—what does it mean?"
* Counting: count three vines, three baskets, seven fat cows, seven skinny cows, seven strong cornstalks, seven straggly cornstalks, eleven brothers, eleven bundles of wheat, eleven stars.
* Colorful coat: name the colors in the coat together, then look back to spot the colors on other pages.
* All shapes and sizes: describe the brothers in terms of shape or size, looking for a tall brother, a short brother, a fat brother, a thin brother.
* Listening: when you see the word on the page, point and make the sound—Snore!

Now that you've read the story . . . what do you remember?

* Who was Joseph?
* Why did his brothers leave Joseph in the well?
* Where did the merchants take Joseph?
* What happened to Joseph in Egypt?
* How did he get out of jail?
* When Joseph saw his father and brothers, how did he feel?

What does the story tell us?
God has a plan for all of us if we listen to him.

Moses
in the
Bulrushes

Once there was a girl called Miriam who lived in Egypt. Her family were Hebrew slaves.

There were many Hebrew slaves in Egypt working for the king.

One day, the king gave an order:
"There are enough Hebrews in Egypt.
There must be no more baby boys."

The king sent soldiers to
all the Hebrew villages.

If they found any baby boys,
they would kill them!

Miriam's mother had a baby boy.
"What are we to do?"
Miriam cried.

Miriam's mother hid the baby in the house and Miriam watched over him.

But when the baby was three months old, he was too big and too noisy to hide in the house any longer.

Miriam's mother found a basket and painted it so that it would not leak. Then she wrapped the baby in a blanket and put him in the basket.

When no one was looking, Miriam and her mother carried the basket down to the river and hid it among the bulrushes.

Miriam's mother hurried back to the house,
leaving Miriam to watch the baby.
All day, Miriam hid nearby to make
sure the baby was safe.

Then, from her hiding place,
Miriam could see some
people coming.

The king's daughter was walking on the riverbank with her servants.

She saw something floating in the bulrushes. "Fetch that for me to see," she told her servant.

The servant brought the little basket to the king's daughter. It floated just like a little boat! The king's daughter looked inside the basket . . . and was amazed.

"It's a baby boy!" she said. The king's daughter lifted the baby from the basket.

The baby began to cry.

“He must be a Hebrew baby,” said the king’s daughter.
“Poor little thing, are you very hungry?”

Just then, Miriam jumped up from her hiding place.

"Shall I fetch someone to feed the baby and look after him for you?" she asked.

"Yes, that's a good idea," said the king's daughter.

Miriam ran to find her mother, and together they hurried down to the river.

"I will pay you to feed this baby and look after him for me," said the king's daughter.

And she handed the baby to his mother.

Miriam and her mother were very happy.

They took the baby back home and cared for him until he was old enough to go to the palace.

The king's daughter was delighted.
"I will bring him up like a son,"
she said. "I will call him Moses."

Next Steps

Look back through the book to find more to talk about and join in with.

* Copy the actions: be a little basket bobbing in the bulrushes.
* Join in with the rhyme: pause to encourage joining in with "Shh, little brother. Be good for Mother!"
* Counting: count five birds and five butterflies.
* Colorful flowers: name the colors of the flowers by the river, then look back to spot the colors on other pages.
* All shapes and sizes: compare the basket and chest that Moses is hidden in as he grows.
* Listening: when you see the word on the page, point and make the sound—Shh! Wah!

Now that you've read the story . . . what do you remember?

* Who was Moses?
* Why did his mother hide him in a basket?
* How old was Moses when he was taken to the river?
* Where did Miriam hide the basket?
* What happened when the king's daughter came to the river?
* When did Moses go to live at the palace?

What does the story tell us?
Sometimes our enemies can become our friends.

David and Goliath

One day, young David was looking after the sheep when he heard his father calling.

"Take this bread and cheese to your brothers," said his father. David's three older brothers were away fighting in King Saul's army.

Taking the bundle, David set off at once.

King Saul's army was camped on a hillside.
On the other hillside, the Philistine army had gathered.

It was an amazing sight!

David searched among the lines of Saul's soldiers. He soon found his three brothers.

Just then, a giant soldier stepped forward
from the Philistine army.

He was so tall,
he towered over
everyone else!

He roared:
"I am Goliath, tall and mighty.
Who is brave enough to fight me?"

Not one of King Saul's soldiers replied.
They were all afraid!

The soldiers talked among themselves.

"The king will give a big prize to whoever kills the mighty giant Goliath," they said.

"What's going on?" young David asked his brothers.

"It has nothing to do with you," they said. "You're just a boy. Go home and look after the sheep."

But David did not go home.
He went to see King Saul in his tent.
"I will fight the giant," said David.

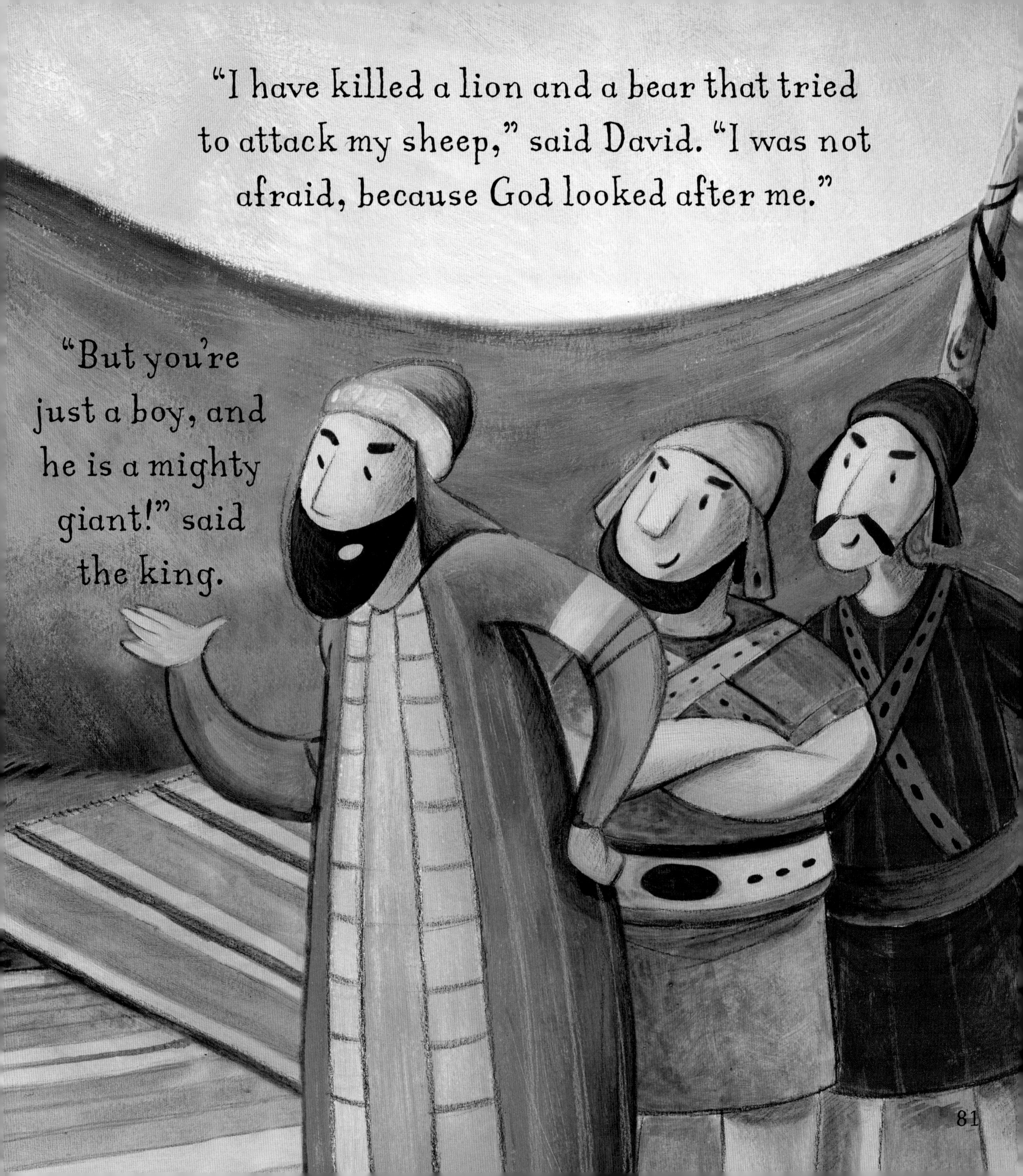
"I have killed a lion and a bear that tried to attack my sheep," said David. "I was not afraid, because God looked after me."
"But you're just a boy, and he is a mighty giant!" said the king.

King Saul gave David a helmet, armor, and a sword.

David put them on. They were much too big!

He tried walking around the tent.

"I can't wear these," he said. "I'm not used to them."

He took them off.

Instead, David took his sling and
his pouch and went down to the stream.

There he found
five smooth stones
and put them in
his pouch.

"My sling was all I needed to fight the lion and the bear," he thought. "God will look after me."

David went down to meet Goliath.
The giant towered over him. He roared:

"I am Goliath, tall and mighty.
Who is brave enough to fight me?"

"I am!" answered David.
"Will you fight me with that stick?"
sneered Goliath.

Goliath was angry!

Goliath lumbered toward David.

David grabbed a stone from his pouch and put it in his sling.

Goliath waved his sword in the air.

David let the stone fly through the air.

The stone hit Goliath in the middle of his forehead. He crashed to the ground.

King Saul's army cheered.
"The mighty Goliath is dead!" they cried.

The Philistine army ran away,

chased by King Saul's soldiers.

Young David was a hero!

Next Steps

Look back through the book to find more to talk about and join in with.

* Copy the actions: make yourself small and short. Pretend you are throwing a shot from a sling. Pretend you have a sword.
* Join in with the rhyme: pause to encourage joining in with "I am Goliath, tall and mighty. Who is brave enough to fight me?"
* Counting: Goliath is nine feet tall. Talk about how high that is—as tall as a basketball hoop or an elephant.
* Colorful tents: name the colors of the tents. Look back through the book to spot the colors on other pages.
* All shapes and sizes: describe the armor that Goliath is wearing. Use words like hard, stiff, shiny, metal, leather.
* Listening: when you see the word on the page, point and make the sound—Clink! Clank! Crack!

Now that you've read the story . . . what do you remember?

* Who was David?
* Why did he go to find his brothers?
* Where did David find King Saul?
* What happened when David tried on the armor?
* How did David have the strength to fight Goliath?
* Why did Goliath crash to the ground?

What does the story tell us?
We can face big problems if God is on our side.

Daniel and the Lions

Daniel was an important man. He was one of three ministers chosen by the king to help him rule the land.

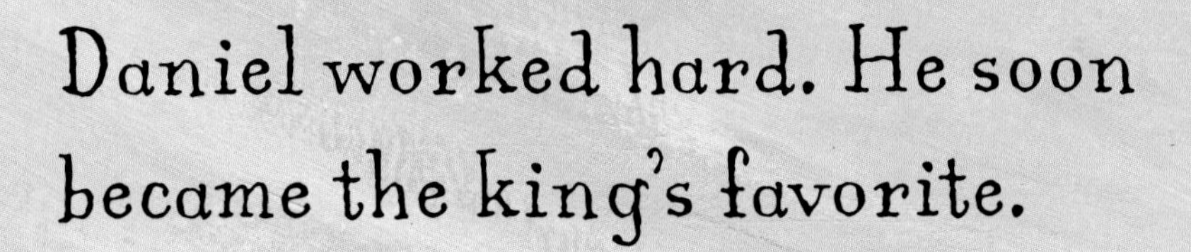

Daniel worked hard. He soon became the king's favorite.

One day, the king decided to put Daniel in charge of everyone.

The other two ministers were angry.

"Why should Daniel be more important than us?" they grumbled.

"He's not even from this land," whispered one.

"And he only praises his own god!" whispered the other.

Together, they came up with a plan to get rid of Daniel.

The two ministers went to see the king. "Oh, King, you are so great!" they cried. "Make a law saying that everyone should praise only you for thirty days!"

The king liked to be praised,
so he listened to them.

"Whoever breaks the law must then
be thrown into the lions' den," they said.
The king agreed to make it the law.

For thirty days, everyone
praised the king.

But Daniel went home,
knelt at the window,
and praised God,
just as he always did.

The two ministers were
spying on Daniel.

When they saw him
praising God,
they went straight
to the king.

"Oh, King, you are so great!" they cried.
"Daniel praised his god. He has broken the law."
When the king heard this he was very sad.

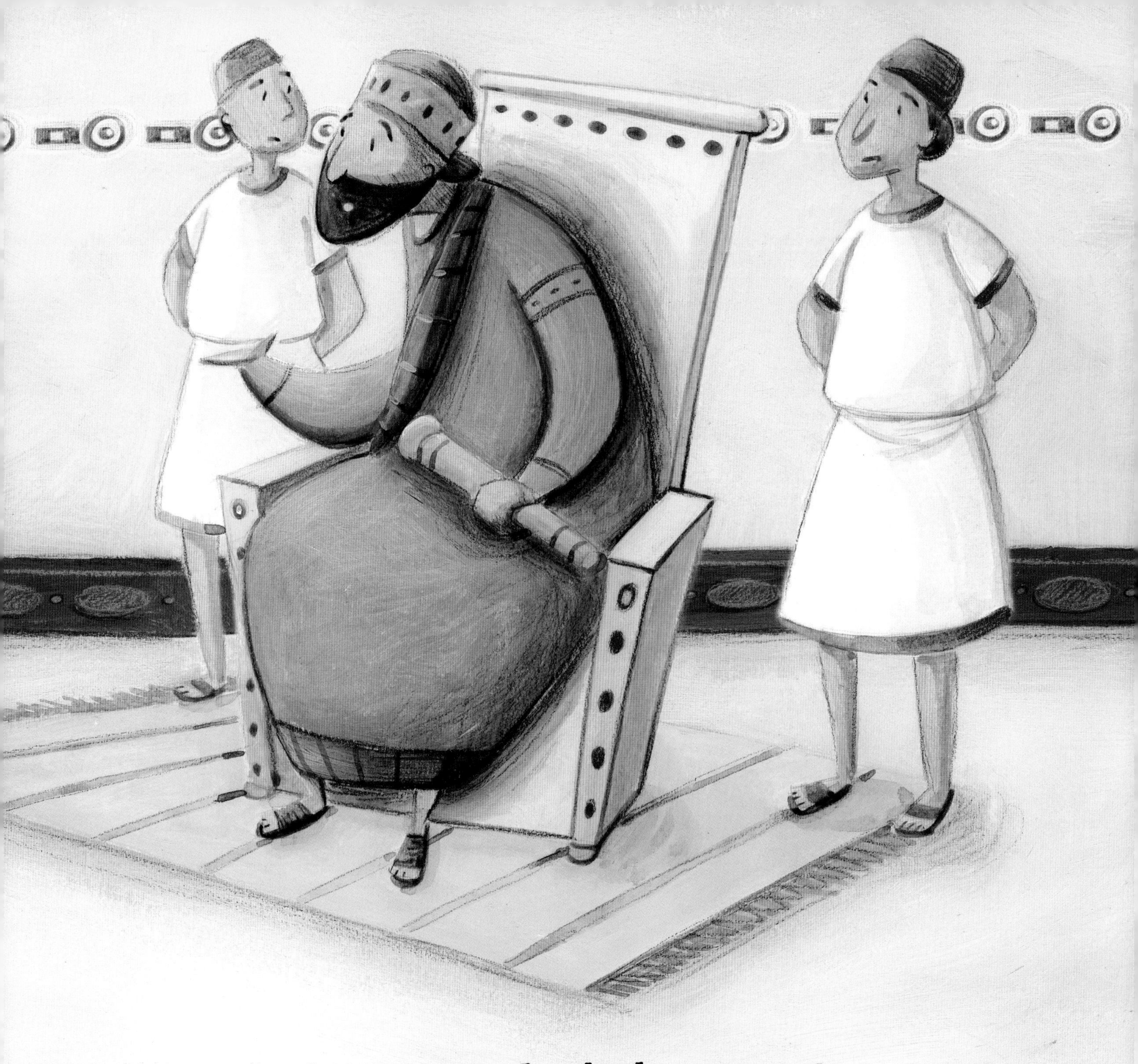

"Whoever breaks the law must then
be thrown into the lions' den," they said.
"The law is the law," sighed the king.

Daniel was taken to the deep, dark den.
Inside, the lions prowled and growled.

Daniel was lowered down into the den.

The lions sniffed and snarled.

The king looked down into the den.
"I hope your God takes care of you,
Daniel," he called sadly.

A big rock was rolled over the den
so that there was no escape.

Daniel sat in the gloomy den.
The lions circled around him.

Then an angel appeared,
and the lions settled down.

The king went back to his palace.

He couldn't eat.

He couldn't work.

He couldn't sleep.

All night long he tossed and turned in his bed.

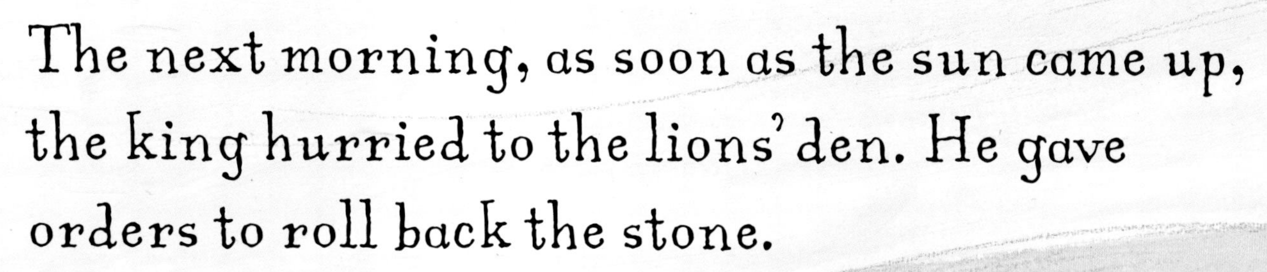

The next morning, as soon as the sun came up, the king hurried to the lions' den. He gave orders to roll back the stone.

"Daniel!" he called. "Has God saved you from the lions?"

"Oh, King, you are great!" called Daniel. "God sent an angel to tame the lions. I am safe."

The king was so happy as Daniel was lifted from the den. There wasn't a mark on him!

The king made a new law.

From that time on, everyone in the land would worship God. "God's law is the law," he said.

Next Steps

Look back through the book to find more to talk about and join in with.

* Copy the actions: pretend you are a lion prowling in the den. Bow down and praise the king.
* Join in with the rhyme: pause to encourage joining in with "Whoever breaks the law must then be thrown into the lions' den."
* Counting: look back through the book to find a pair of soldiers and a pair of lions.
* Colorful crown: name the colors in the king's crown together, then look back to spot the colors on other pages.
* All shapes and sizes: compare the two ministers and talk about tall, short, thin, fat.
* Listening: when you see the word on the page, point and make the sound–Grrr!

Now that you've read the story . . . what do you remember?

* Who was Daniel?
* Why was he the king's favorite?
* Why did Daniel pray to God?
* Where did Daniel end up?
* What happened when Daniel was in the lions' den?
* How did Daniel get out of the den?

What does the story tell us?

We don't have to be afraid of scary things, because God is looking after us.

Jonah and the Big Fish

Most of the time, Jonah was a good man.

So one day, God
asked Jonah
to do a job for him.

"Go to the city of Nineveh,
and deliver a message for me."

But Jonah didn't want to go to Nineveh.
Instead he ran away.

Jonah found a boat to take him far away from Nineveh.
He hid belowdecks and fell fast asleep.

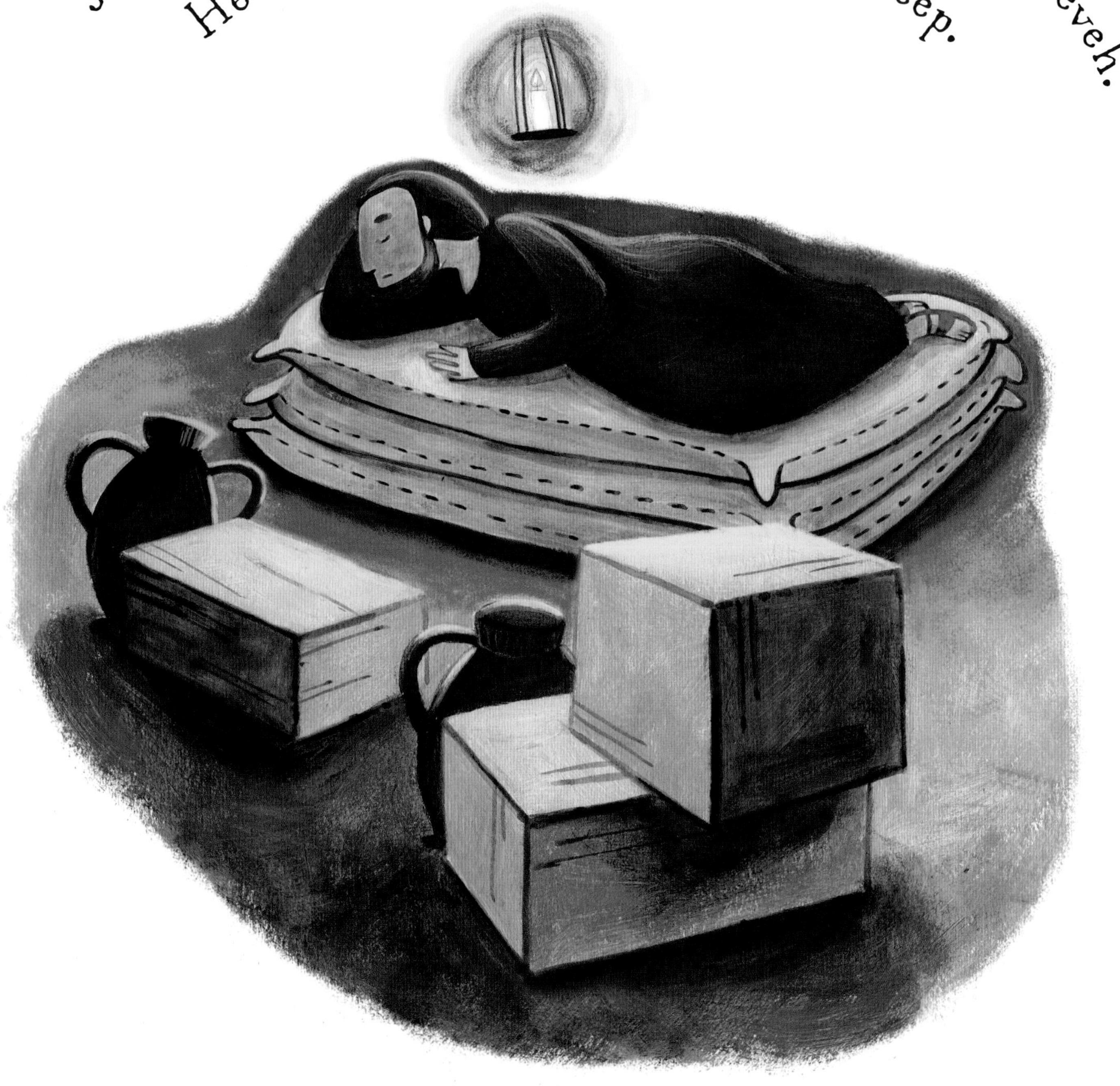

As he slept, the wind blew and the waves crashed.

A storm rocked the boat, and still Jonah slept!

The captain of the boat came to wake Jonah.

"How can you sleep in this storm!" cried the captain. "Get up and say a prayer!"

The boat rocked this way and that way.
The sailors were all afraid.
"Throw the cargo overboard!"
the captain cried.

But it was no use. The storm grew wilder and wilder.
"It's my fault," said Jonah. "I didn't do as God asked me."
The sailors were shocked and afraid.

"God is angry with me," said Jonah.
"Throw me overboard and the storm will stop."

Now the sailors didn't really want to throw Jonah overboard. They prayed and prayed. But still the storm rocked the boat.

Finally, they threw Jonah—SPLOSH!—into the waves.

SPLOSH!

And the storm stopped!

Jonah sank through the water
deeper
and
deeper.

Jonah began to pray:
"I'm sinking down!
Don't let me drown!"

Then he saw a great big fish swim toward him.
The fish opened its mouth wide, wider–
and swallowed him
in one gulp.
GULP!

Jonah sat inside the fish's belly.
He had plenty of time to think. He had run away from God and was punished.

He had prayed to God
and was saved. Now Jonah thanked God, and God forgave him.

After three days, the big fish burped.

Jonah shot out of its mouth and landed on a beach!

This time, Jonah went to the city of Nineveh to deliver God's message.

The people there were wicked. They didn't listen to God either.

For three days Jonah walked through the city, calling, "Mend your ways in forty days or Nineveh will be destroyed!"

When they heard Jonah's message from God, the people of Nineveh were shocked.

Even the king of Nineveh was shocked.

They had forgotten that God was watching them.

They were very sorry that they had been bad and decided to be good from then on.

So God forgave them.

Jonah sat on a hill outside Nineveh and waited for the city to be destroyed.

But it was very hot and nothing happened. Jonah became very grumpy.

God said to Jonah,
"Why are you grumpy?
I forgave you because I
love you. And I forgave
the people of Nineveh
because I love them."

And finally, Jonah understood that
God's love was big enough for everyone.

Next Steps

Look back through the book to find more to talk about and join in with.

* Copy the actions: pretend you are in a boat being tossed by the waves. Pretend you are a fish. Make a wave action with your hand and arm.
* Join in with the rhyme: pause to encourage joining in with "I'm sinking down! Don't let me drown!"
* Counting: Jonah is inside the big fish for three days. Nineveh has forty days to mend its ways. Talk about how long three days is and how long forty days is.
* Colorful fish: name the colors of the fish together, then look back to spot the colors on other pages.
* All shapes and sizes: compare the big fish with the other fish on the page. How big is the big fish compared with the boat?
* Listening: when you see the word on the page, point and make the sound—Splosh! Gulp!

Now that you've read the story . . . what do you remember?

* Who was Jonah?
* Why did he run away to sea?
* Where did Jonah end up when he was thrown into the sea?
* How did Jonah get out of the big fish?
* What happened when Jonah got to Nineveh?
* Why did Jonah become grumpy?

What does the story tell us?
If we do the wrong thing, God will show us the right thing to do.